MW00389760

WORKBOO

My ABC Storybook

Beat Eisele

Catherine Yang Eisele

Stephen M. Hanlon

Rebecca York Hanlon

Barbara Hojel

Longman

My ABC Storybook
Workbook

Pearson Education, 10 Bank Street, White Plains, NY 10606

Vice president, director of publishing: Allen Ascher
Publisher: Anne Stribling
Senior development editor: Yoko Mia Hirano
Assistant editor: Iris Candelaria
Vice president, director of design and production: Rhea Banker
Executive managing editor: Linda Moser
Production manager: Alana Zdinak
Senior production editor: Mike Kemper
Director of manufacturing: Patrice Fraccio
Senior manufacturing buyer: Edie Pullman
Cover design: Rhea Banker and Lisa Donovan
Illustrators: Chris Reed and Mena Dolobowsky
Art direction and production: Pearson Education Development Group

ISBN: 0-13-019774-2

5 6 7 8 9 10-BAH-05 04 03 02

Contents

Find. Say. Color.

Draw and Color. Say.

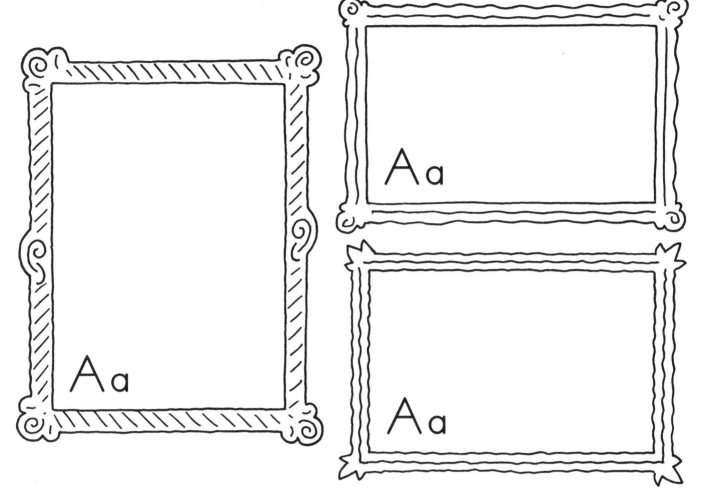

Aa

Aa

Aa

Write.

A A

a a

Find. Say. Color.

Match. Say. Color.

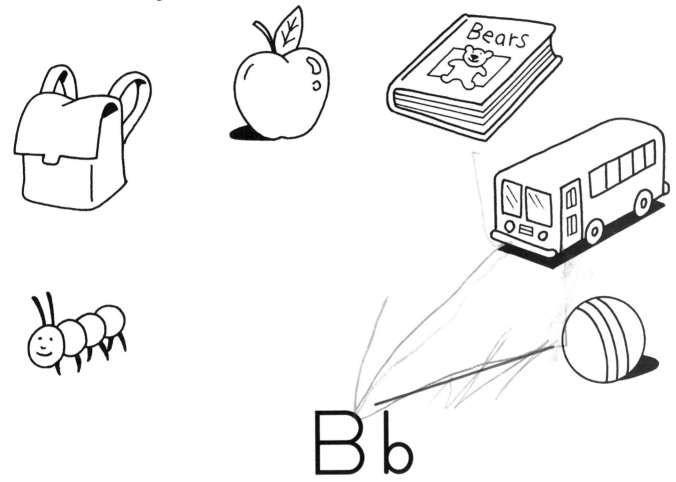

B b

Write.

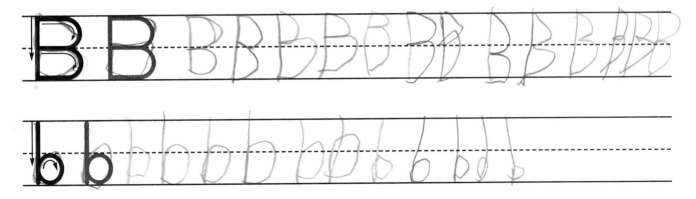

Find. Say. Color.

Draw a path. Say. Color.

Write.

C C

c c

Review: Aa, Bb, Cc

Trace. Draw and color.

  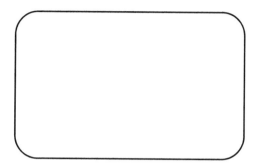

  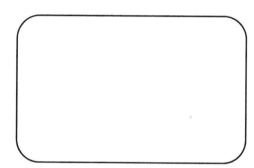

  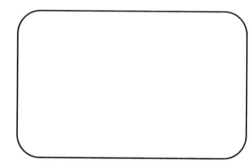

Write.

Talk Time

Listen. Draw and color.

Andy

Becky

Carla

Don

I am _____ .

Find. Say. Color.

Point. Say. Color.

Write.

D

d

Find. Say. Color.

Match. Say. Color.

Write.

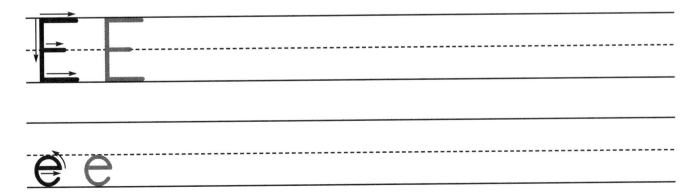

Find. Say. Color.

Follow. Say. Color.

Write.

Review: Dd, Ee, Ff

Color. Say. Write.

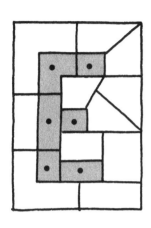   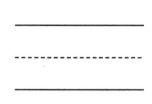

  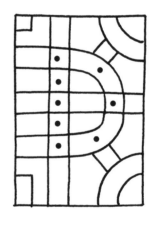

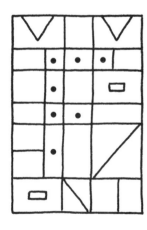  

Talk Time

 **Listen. Say.**

a.

b.

c.
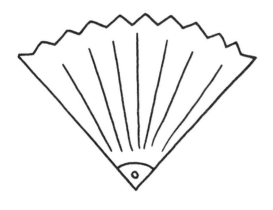

d.
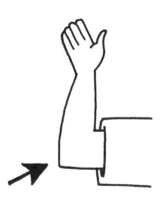

e.

f.

Find. Say. Color.

Point. Say. Color.

Write.

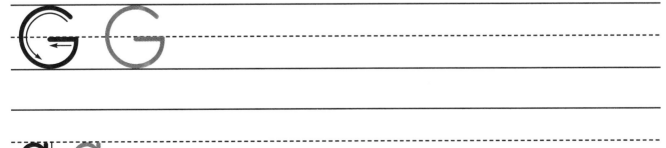

Find. Say. Color.

Draw and color. Say.

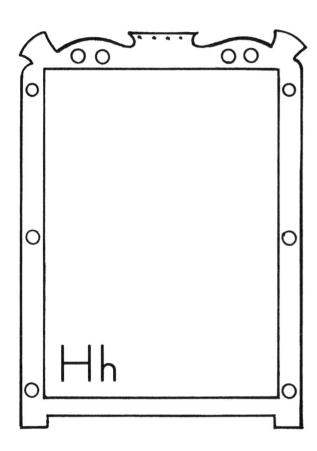

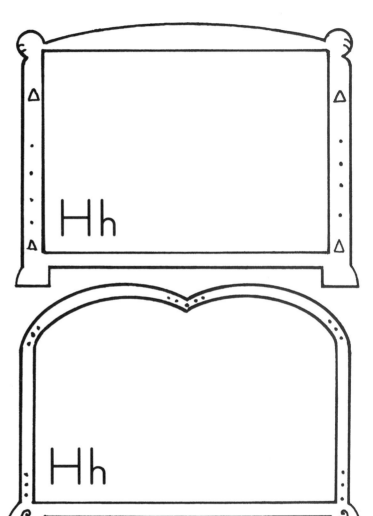

Write.

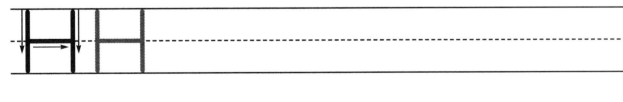

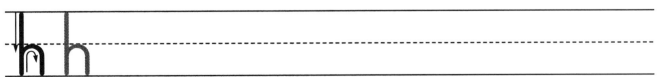

Find. Say. Color.

a.

b.

c.

Write.

Review: Gg, Hh, Ii

Trace. Match. Say.

Talk Time

Listen. Color.

Find. Say. Color.

Match. Say. Color.

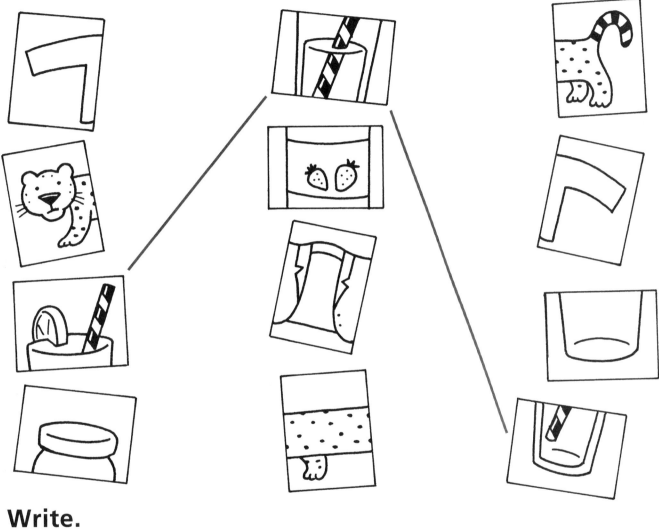

Write.

Find. Say. Color.

Draw a path. Say. Color.

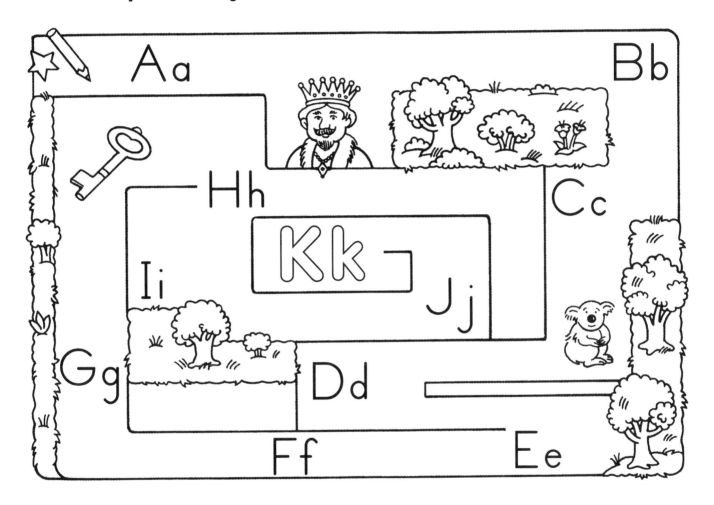

Write.

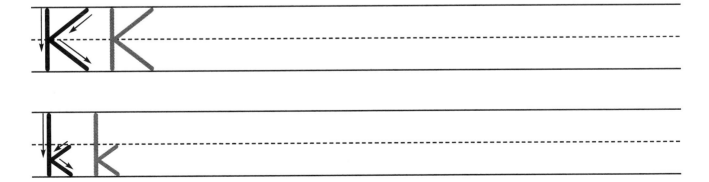

Find. Say. Color.

🎧 **Listen. Say. Circle. Color.**

Write.

Review: Jj, Kk, Ll

Point. Match. Say.

Talk Time

Draw. Say. Color.

Find. Say. Color.

Draw a path. Say. Color.

Write.

M M

m m

Find. Say. Color.

This Way

Don

 Listen. Circle. Color.

Write.

N N

n n

Find. Say. Color.

Match. Say. Color.

Write.

Review: Mm, Nn, Oo

Say. Write.

N n

Talk Time

🎧 Listen. Color.

Find. Say. Color.

 Listen. Circle.

a.

b.

c.

d.

Write.

Find. Say. Color.

Draw a path. Say. Color.

Write.

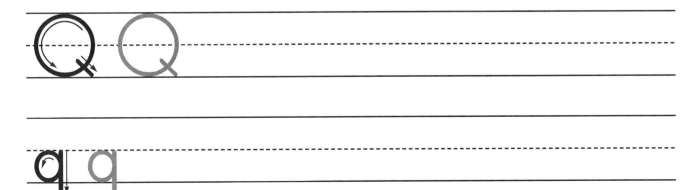

Find. Say. Color.

Point. Say. Color.

Write.

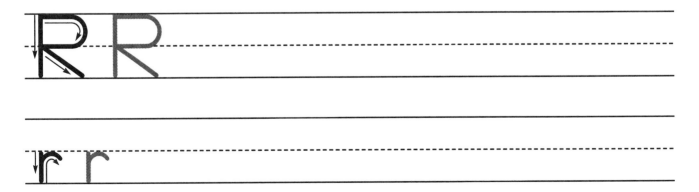

Review: Pp, Qq, Rr

Look. Guess. Write.

quilt	_rabbit_	_ring_
Qq		
pizza	_peach_	_penguin_
plant	_quail_	_rope_

Talk Time

Count. Say. Color.

3

_____

_____

_____

_____

Find. Say. Color.

Match. Say. Color.

Write.

S S

s s

Find. Say. Color.

Draw a path. Say. Color.

Write.

Find. Say. Color.

Connect the dots.

Write.

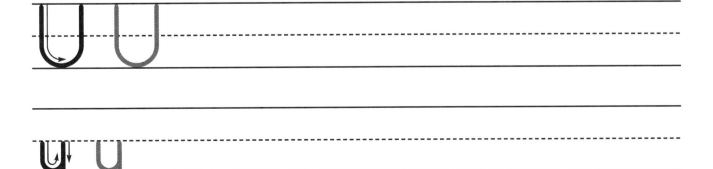

Review: Ss, Tt, Uu

Match. Say.

Talk Time

 Listen. Circle.

1.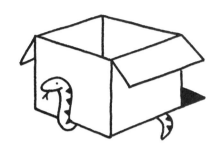

2.

3.

4.

Find. Say. Color.

Match. Say.

V v

Write.

V V

V V

Find. Say. Color.

Draw and color. Say.

Write.

W W

W W

Find. Say. Color.

Connect the dots. Say.

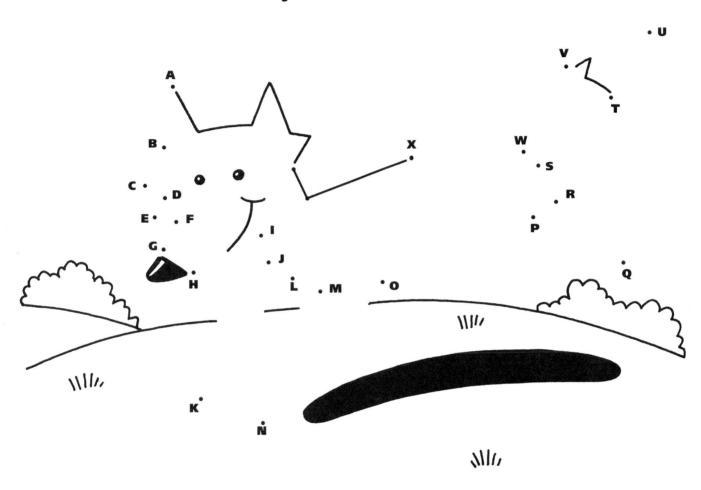

Write.

Review: Vv, Ww, Xx

Draw and color. Say.

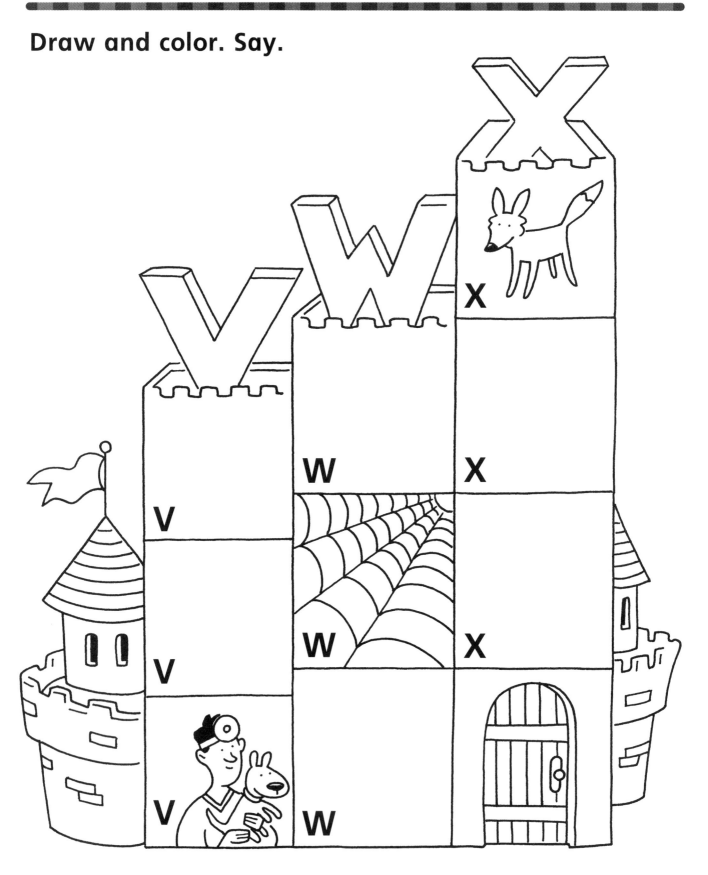

Talk Time

 Listen. Circle.

1.

2.

3.

4.

Find. Say. Color.

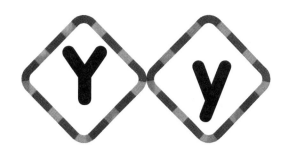

Match. Say. Color.

a.
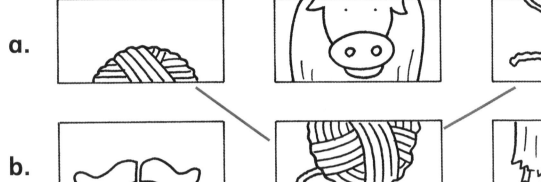

b.

c.

d.
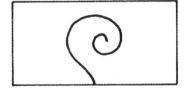

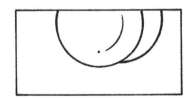

Write.

Find. Say. Color.

Draw paths. Say. Color.

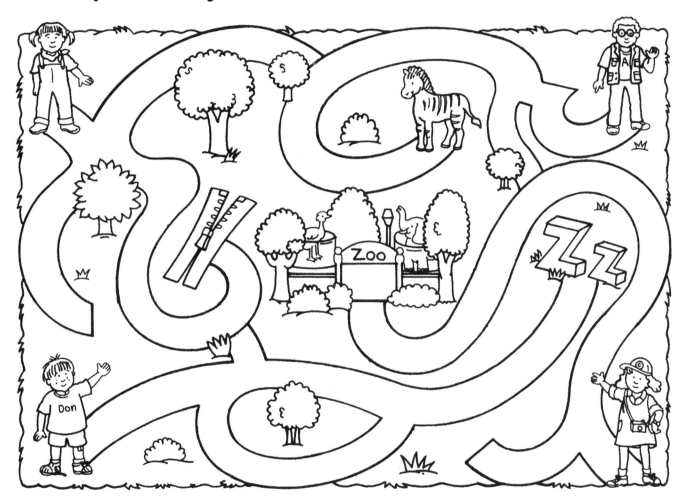

Write.

Z z

Z z

Review: Yy, Zz

Circle. Say.

Connect the dots. Color.

A B   D   E | K   L   M
J | Z
               | Y   X   N
               | w
               | • O
        C |
               |
  I   • F | V   P   Q   R
               |
  H   • G | U   T   S

Talk Time

1.

2.

3.

4.

Alphabet Practice

Say. Write.

Alphabet
Practice (continued)

Shapes

Say. Color.

◯ yellow   □ red   ▭ green   △ blue

Days of the Week

Trace. Draw.

Monday

Tuesday

Wednesday

Thursday

Friday

Saturday

Sunday

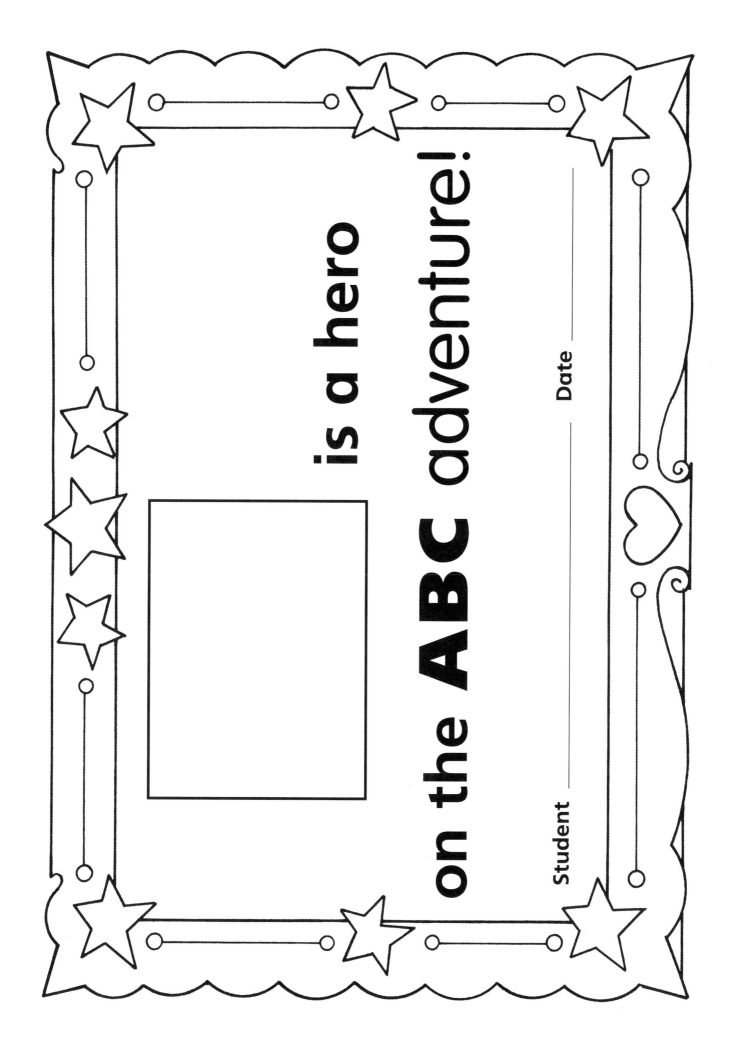

is a hero

on the **ABC** adventure!

Student

Date